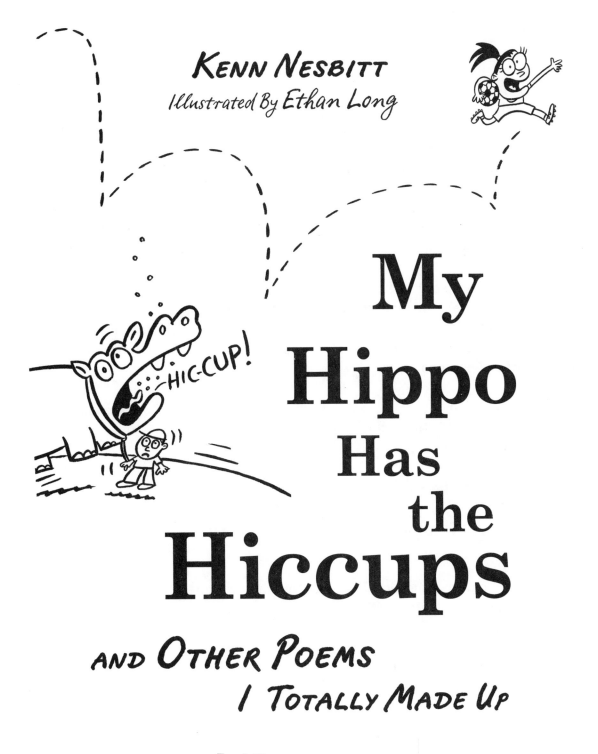

KENN NESBITT
Illustrated By Ethan Long

HIC-CUP!

My
Hippo
Has
the
Hiccups

AND OTHER POEMS
I TOTALLY MADE UP

Copyright © 2009 by Kenn Nesbitt
"Willie's Wart," "Mirror, Mirror," "Melinda McKnight," and "Meat Loaf"
    © Kenn Nesbitt and Linda Knaus
Cover and internal design © 2009 by Sourcebooks, Inc.
Front cover design by Stewart Williams
Cover and internal illustrations by Ethan Long

Published by Sourcebooks Jabberwocky, an imprint of Sourcebooks, Inc.
P.O. Box 4410, Naperville, Illinois 60567-4410
(630) 961-3900
Fax: (630) 961-2168
www.sourcebooks.com

Library of Congress Cataloging-in-Publication Data

Nesbitt, Kenn.
  My hippo has the hiccups : and other poems I totally made up / by Kenn
Nesbitt ; illustrated by Ethan Long.
      p. cm.
  1. Children's poetry, American. I. Long, Ethan, ill. II. Title.
  PS3614.E47M9 2009
  811'.6—dc22
                          2008048478

Printed and bound in the United States of America.
            LB 10 9 8 7 6 5 4 3 2 1

To Madison and Max

CONTENTS

POEM TITLE	PAGE	((💿))

POEM TITLE	PAGE	

POEM TITLE	PAGE	

POEM TITLE	PAGE	

POEM TITLE	PAGE	

TRACK LIST

TRACK LIST, CONTINUED

MY HIPPO HAS THE HICCUPS

My hippo has the hiccups
and his hiccups shake the ground.
The floor is always rumbling
when my hippo is around.

I bought him at the pet store,
but I missed a small detail.
I didn't see the sign said,
"Hiccupotamus for sale."

HIC-CUP!

TODAY'S MY FAVORITE HOLIDAY

Today's my favorite holiday,
a day to sing and dance and play,
a day to laugh and jump and run,
a day for having loads of fun.

Today's the day I celebrate.
I'm overjoyed. I'm feeling great!
I'll throw a party, have a ball,
invite a friend, invite them all!

2

We'll play a game. We'll play a sport.
We'll frolic, rollick, romp, cavort.
We'll celebrate all over town.
We'll party till the sun goes down.

Another favorite holiday
just happened only yesterday.
And, yes, tomorrow, strange but true,
will surely be my favorite too.

You want to know how there could be
so many holidays for me?
It's simple. See, to qualify,
a day just has to end in "Y."

3

TODAY i WROTE THiS POEM

Today I wrote this poem,
but I wonder if it's good.
It doesn't have the things
my teacher says a poem should.

It doesn't share the feelings
I have deep inside of me.
It hasn't any metaphors
and not one simile.

It's missing any narrative.
Alliteration too.
It isn't an acrostic,
diamanté, or haiku.

There's nothing that's personified.
It doesn't have a plot.
I'm pretty sure that rhyming
is the only thing it's got.

It sure was fun to write it,
and I think it's long enough.
It's just too bad it's missing
all that great poetic stuff.

I put it on my teacher's desk
and, wow, she made a fuss.
She handed back my poem
with an A++++!

MY POEM

A++++

5

MY ROBOT'S MISBEHAVING

My robot's misbehaving.
It won't do as I say.
It will not dust the furniture
or put my toys away.

My robot never helps me
with homework or my chores.
It doesn't do my laundry
and neglects to clean the floors.

It claims it can't cook dinner.
It never makes my bed.
No matter what I ask of it,
it simply shakes its head.

My robot must be broken.
I'll need to get another.
Until that day, I have to say,
I'm glad I have my mother.

i THiNK MY DAD iS DRACULA

I think my dad is Dracula.
I know that sounds insane,
but listen for a moment and
allow me to explain.

We don't live in a castle,
and we never sleep in caves.
But, still, there's something weird
about the way my dad behaves.

I never see him go out
in the daytime when it's light.
He sleeps all day till evening,
then he leaves the house at night.

He comes home in the morning
saying, "Man, I'm really dead!"
He kisses us good night, and then
by sunrise he's in bed.

My mom heard my suspicion
and she said, "You're not too swift.
Your father's not a vampire.
He just works the graveyard shift."

1 CRAZY PLACE

Instead of having streets with names
like Broadway, Park, or Main,
our town has streets like Hyper Drive,
No Way, and Lois Lane.

We have a street named Rowboat Row,
and one called Winfirst Place,
plus Up-Your Alley, Endless Loop,
and even Pencil Trace.

We have the Lolo Highway
and a street called Running Walk.
Another one named Circle Square
is just around the block.

There's Ginger Route, and Tennis Court,
and also Upson Downs.
It's fair to say we have
the most unusual of towns.

So come and find Your Happy Place;
it's right near Silly's Mile.
We hope you'll like our town so much
you'll move to Stayaw Aisle.

i WENT TO THE BARBER

I went to the barber.
He cut off my hair,
which would have been great,
but he didn't stop there.

He slipped with his scissors.
He snipped with his shears,
and cut off my eyebrows
and both of my ears.

I jumped in my seat
causing several more slips;
he cut off my nose
and my cheeks and my lips.

With one final slip-up
he cut off my head,
and that is the reason
I ended up dead.

So kids, if your dad tells you,
"You need a trim,"
just pull out this poem
and show it to him.

As soon as he reads this
I'm willing to bet
that *that's* the last haircut
that you'll ever get.

A FISH IN A SPACESHIP

A fish in a spaceship is flying through school.
A dinosaur's dancing on top of a stool.
The library's loaded with orange baboons,
in purple tuxedos with bows and balloons.
The pigs on the playground are having a race
while pencils parade in their linens and lace.
As camels do cartwheels and elephants fly,
bananas are baking a broccoli pie.
A hundred gorillas are painting the walls,
while robots on rockets careen through the halls.
Tomatoes are teaching in all of the classes.
Or maybe, just maybe, I need some new glasses.

MY PARENTS ARE MAKING ME CRAZY

My parents are making me crazy.
They're driving me utterly mad.
I'm mental because of my mother.
I'm losing it thanks to my dad.

My mom tells me, "Go do your homework,"
and dad's yelling, "Vacuum the floors!"
Then mom says, "Turn off the TV now,"
and dad hollers, "Finish your chores!"

With all of their grousing and griping,
my brain is beginning to hurt.
My dad's shouting, "Clean up the kitchen!"
My mom's saying, "Tuck in your shirt!"

I feel like I'm losing my marbles.
If I go bananas today,
then please give this note to my parents
when the funny farm takes me away.

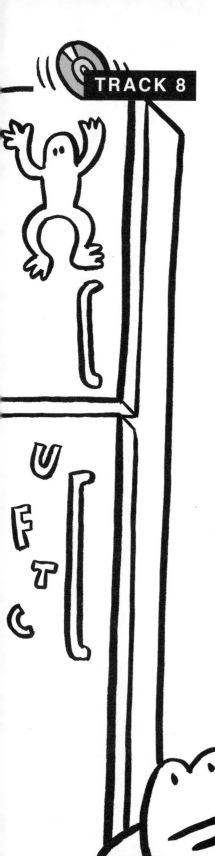

FRANK THE FROG COLLECTOR

I'm Frank the frog collector,
and I'm happy to report
my collection's nearly finished;
I have frogs of every sort.

I record them in my journal
so that every single frog
is accounted for completely
with an entry in my log.

I have hundreds, maybe thousands,
of amphibians at home.
I have frogs of quilted fabric.
I have frogs of gleaming chrome.

I have frogs of painted porcelain,
and frogs of brass and tin.
I have frogs you open up
to find another frog within.

There are small magnetic tree frogs
clinging gently to the fridge,
and Louisiana bullfrogs
on a plastic bayou bridge.

I have frogs on ancient bicycles
with shiny silver bells.
I have frogs proposing marriage
to their froggy mademoiselles.

You'll see frogs ascending ladders.
You'll see frogs descending stairs,
yes, and frogs reclining dreamily
in comfy leather chairs.

I have frogs with pink umbrellas.
I have frogs engrossed in books.
Even frogs that dangle fishing poles
in nonexistent brooks.

My abode is filled with frogs
from top to bottom, front to back.
There are frogs in every corner,
every crevice, every crack.

There is only one that's missing;
just one blank space in my log.
So I'm begging, mom and dad,
can I please have a *real* frog?

IZZY O'RAINTY

I's Izzy O'Rainty.
I ain't not bizzare.
I is how I ain't
and I ain't how I are.

I wasn't not never
the way that I was.
And now I don't never
not do what I does.

At being not me
I is truly a whiz.
I is what I's not
and I ain't what I is.

I wouldn't not never
not do what I won't.
Whatever I can do
I certainly don't.

I isn't not happy.
I has no complaint.
I's perfect not being
just not how I ain't.

I is how I are when
I ain't how I be.
I's Izzy O'Rainty.
I's not really me.

i TAUGHT MY CAT TO CLEAN MY ROOM

I taught my cat to clean my room,
to use a bucket, brush, and broom,
to dust my clock and picture frames,
and pick up all my toys and games.

He puts my pants and shirts away,
and makes my bed and, I would say,
it seems to me it's only fair
he puts away my underwear.

In fact, I think he's got it made.
I'm not as happy with our trade.
He may pick up my shoes and socks,
but I clean out his litter box.

ALPHABET BREAK

I'm learning all my ABC's.
I'm good at D, E, F, and G's.

I've mastered H and I and J,
and memorized the letter K.

I've studied L, M, N, and O,
but now I really have to go.

Before I learn one more, you see,
I really must get up to P.

DEXTER MCDWYER

I'm Dexter McDwyer, an excellent liar.
I never say anything true.
Which means I'm implying I'm probably lying,
so I don't believe me. Do you?

STEVE THE SUPERHERO

He's Steve the superhero,
and you simply won't believe
the powers he possesses
by merely being Steve.

His smile can crack a mirror
and his breath can make you faint.
And when he takes his socks off
it's been known to peel the paint.

The power in his underarms
can make a grown man cry.
A single burp can make you want
to crawl away and die.

The bad guys know it's hopeless,
so they all get up and leave
whenever they get wind of him—
the superhero Steve.

SNAiL RACE

Two smug and sluggish snails, one day,
were racing down the street.
The first exclaimed, "You'll lose this race,
for I cannot be beat."

The second said, "I think we'll see
it's you who comes in last."
He bragged, "Of all the snails in town,
I'm fastest of the fast."

The first replied, "You're much too slow
to best the likes of me."
The second gloated heartily.
"Just wait," he said, "you'll see."

They inched along the roadway
as they boasted of their speed.
Their slowness was identical
and neither took the lead.

The two approached the finish
at the same unhurried pace,
a half an inch away from
the conclusion of the race.

They never crossed the finish line
for, as events transpired,
a car drove by that moment
and they must have gotten tired.

i'M ABSOLUTELY FULL TONiGHT

I'm absolutely full tonight.
I couldn't eat another bite.
I couldn't eat a half a bean
or even taste a tangerine.
I couldn't lick a lettuce leaf
or bite the slightest bit of beef.
I couldn't polish off a pea
or sip a single drop of tea
or nibble on a nanogram
of pickled ham or candied yam
or lamb or clam or jam or Spam.
Yes, that's how truly full I am.
To even think of eating more
would leave me lying on the floor
and surely make my stomach hurt
unless, of course, you've got dessert.

MY DOG IS NOT THE SMARTEST DOG

My dog is not the smartest dog alive.
He seems to think that two and two make five.
He's sure Japan's the capital of France.
He says that submarines know how to dance.

My dog declares that tigers grow on trees.
He argues only antelopes eat cheese.
He tells me that he's twenty-nine feet tall,
then adds that ants are good at basketball.

He claims to own a mansion on the moon;
a palace that he bought from a baboon.
He swears the sun is made of candy bars,
and says he's seen bananas play guitars.

It seems to me my dog is pretty dense.
He talks a lot, but doesn't make much sense.
Although I love my dog with all my heart,
I have to say, he isn't very smart.

BRADLEY BEARD IS RATHER WEIRD

Bradley Beard is rather weird;
the strangest kid around.
He grabs his socks and pulls them up
and rises off the ground.

He'll tug on his suspenders
or he'll yank upon his hair,
and suddenly he's levitating,
floating in the air.

He must be filled with helium,
or may be awfully strong.
Regardless, though, it's fun to see him
hovering along.

But do not envy Bradley Beard;
he has to watch his weight,
for if he ever gains a pound
he'll cease to levitate.

And if he doesn't eat enough
on any given day,
then Bradley Beard, who's rather weird,
will simply float away.

i DREAMED i WAS RiDiNG A ZEBRA

I dreamed I was riding a zebra
with curly pink hair on his head,
and when I woke up in the morning
that zebra was there in my bed.

I rode into school on my zebra.
It caused all the teachers to scream.
But then I was slightly embarrassed
to find it was still just a dream.

I woke up again in my bedroom,
and saw with relief and a laugh,
I don't have a pink-headed zebra.
I guess I'll just ride the giraffe.

THE CONTENTS OF MY DESK

A nail.
A nickle.
A snail.
A pickle.
A twisted-up slinky.
A ring for my pinky.
A blackened banana.
A love note from Hannah.
My doodles of rockets.
The lint from my pockets.
A forklike utensil.
But, sorry...
no pencil.

MY SISTER THINKS SHE'S SANTA CLAUS

My sister thinks she's Santa Claus.
It's really kind of cute.
She likes to shout out, "Ho, Ho, Ho!"
and wears a bright red suit.

She carries lots of toys around
inside a great big sack,
and keeps her eight pet reindeer
with her sleigh out in the back.

She even has a workshop
where she makes a lot of noise
directing all the Elves who help
by making brand-new toys.

Then, once a year, on Christmas Eve,
she flies off in her sleigh
delivering her gifts around the world
for Christmas Day.

She'd make a perfect Santa
which is why it's just too bad
my sister can't be Santa Claus;
see, Santa is our dad.

MY BUNNY LiES OVER MY DOGGY

(to the tune of "My Bonnie Lies over the Ocean")

My pets were out practicing football.
My frog intercepted a pass.
My cat and my dog and my bunny
then tackled him flat on the grass.

My bunny lies over my doggy.
My doggie lies over my cat.
My cat is on top of my froggy,
and that's why my froggy is flat.

CHORUS
Green splat. Green splat.
Oh, that's why my froggy is flat, like that.
Green splat. Green splat.
Oh, that's why my froggy is flat.

My froggy's as flat as a pancake.
A paper-thin froggy's the worst.
He still enjoys flies for his dinner,
but I have to flatten them first.

CHORUS

If you see your pets playing football,
it's best if you bring them inside,
or you may end up with a froggy
who's flattened and seven feet wide.

CHORUS

WILLIE'S WART

Willie had a stubborn wart
upon his middle toe.
Regardless, though, of what he tried,
the wart refused to go.

So Willie went and visited
his family foot physician,
who instantly agreed
it was a stubborn wart condition.

The doctor tried to squeeze the wart.
He tried to twist and turn it.
He tried to scrape and shave the wart.
He tried to boil and burn it.

He poked it with a pair of tongs.
He pulled it with his tweezers.
He held it under heat lamps
and he crammed it into freezers.

Regrettably these treatments
were of very little use.
He looked at it and sputtered,
"Ach! I cannot get it loose!

"I'll have to get some bigger tools
to help me to dissect it.
I'll need to pound and pummel it,
bombard it and inject it."

He whacked it with a hammer
and he yanked it with a wrench.
He seared it with a welding torch
despite the nasty stench.

He drilled it with a power drill.
He wrestled it with pliers.
He zapped it with a million volts
from large electric wires.

He blasted it with gamma rays,
besieged it with corrosives,
assaulted it with dynamite
and nuclear explosives.

He hit the wart with everything
but when the smoke had cleared,
poor Willie's stubborn wart remained,
and Willie'd disappeared.

i PLAYED A GAME

I played a game.
I rode my bike.
I had a snack.
I took a hike.
I read a book.
I watched TV.

I built a fort.
I climbed a tree.
I surfed the web.
I played guitar.
I caught a bug
inside a jar.

I called my friends.
I dug a hole.
I kicked a ball.
I scored a goal.
I had a swim.
I learned to skate.

I played with toys.
I stayed up late.
It's fair to say
I do like school,
but even more, though,
weekends rule!

LEARNING LANGUAGES

My mom and dad learned Latin
many years ago in school.
My brother's taking Spanish,
which he thinks is pretty cool.

My sister studies French
because she loves the way they speak.
But I just like computers
so I'm learning Ancient Geek.

MY MOUSE IS RATHER FOND OF CHEESE

My mouse is rather fond of cheese
from hereabouts or overseas,
like cheddars, Parmesans, and Bries
in brick or wheel or ball.

He'll eat ricotta, feta too,
plus Gorgonzola, Gouda, bleu,
in sandwiches or cheese fondue.
My mouse will eat them all.

He'll have Havarti for a snack,
a slice or two, and then a stack
of mozzarella, Swiss, and jack.
He thinks they're oh so nice.

But though my mouse and I agree
we both enjoy a tasty Brie,
I'll miss my mouse because, you see,
my cat is fond of mice.

MYTHICAL MONSTER PARTY

The monsters are having a mythical ball;
a party like never before.
Their musical madness is rocking the hall
as the creatures are crowding the floor.

The Sirens are singing symphonious songs.
The Centaurs are ringing a chime.
The Giants are jumping and banging their gongs
while the Titans are waltzing in time.

The Sphinxes swing saxophones this way and that.
The Harpies perform on their harps.
The Sea Monsters sing all the notes that are flat
as the Serpents are sounding the sharps.

The Minotaurs strum on their mandolin strings.
The Dragons are pounding their drums.
Medusa can't use any musical things
so she hangs with the Hydras and hums.

The Tritons are rapping, the Chimeras chant,
and Cerberus croons with them all.
The Cyclops would dance but he thinks that he can't
so he just keeps his eye on the ball.

SHELLEY SELLERS

Shelley Sellers sells her shells
at Shelley's Seashell Cellars.
She sells shells (and she sure sells!)
to smelly seashore dwellers.

Smelly dwellers shop the sales
at Shelley's seashell store.
Salty sailors stop their ships
for seashells by the shore.

Shelley's shop, a shabby shack,
so sandy, salty, smelly,
still sells shells despite the smells;
a swell shell shop for Shelley.

i THOUGHT iT WAS A BASKETBALL

I thought it was a basketball.
Instead it was a globe.
What should have been a scooter
was pajamas and a robe.

The box I thought had race cars
or a new computer game,
turned out to be a sweater
and an empty picture frame.

The drum set that I asked you for
turned out to be a desk,
and all the other gifts I got
were equally grotesque.

So Santa, when you've made your rounds,
if you have time enough,
I hope you'll please come back;
you gave me someone else's stuff!

I'M DIGGING A TUNNEL TO CHINA

I'm digging a tunnel to China.
A vertical shaft in the ground.
A passage bisecting the planet.
A cavern so deep, it's profound.

I've picked out the perfect location.
I've started out back in the yard.
I think it may take me all summer.
I'm certain the work will be hard.

I'm using a coal-miner's helmet
for working in darkness or shade.
My work boots are perfectly suited
for breaking the earth with my spade.

I'll pummel the rocks with a pickax.
I'll dredge up the dirt with my hands.
I'll suction the sludgy deposits.
I'll scoop out the pebbles and sands.

I'll shovel out mountains of gravel.
I'll excavate acres of soil.
I'll dig till I feel like collapsing
from endless and backbreaking toil.

I'll dig till I reach molten magma
and smash through the Earth's outer crust,
then don my protective equipment,
as onward and downward I thrust.

My tunnel will come out in China,
or maybe Tibet or Japan,
and people will come from all over
to witness its breathtaking span.

And when my achievement's completed
I'll dust myself off with a grin,
then step to the edge of my tunnel
and throw all my Brussels sprouts in.

(i'M ALWAYS iN PARENTHESES)

(I'm always in parentheses)
(which makes me hard to hear)
(regardless if I'm yelling loud)
(or if you're leaning near.)

(It sounds as if I'm whispering.)
(My voice is just a squeak,)
(and even if I scream and shout)
(it comes out soft and meek.)

(Parentheses imprison me.)
(They hold me like a jail.)
(I try to break these tiny curves)
(but every time I fail.)

(I'm sick of these parentheses,)
(these little muffling arcs.)
I WANT TO BE IN CAPITALS
WITH EXCLAMATION MARKS!!!!

MY FATHER LOOKS LiKE FRANKENSTEIN

My father looks like Frankenstein.
My mom looks like Godzilla.
My brother looks like Dracula.
My sister, Vampirella.

My family is the scariest
in this entire city.
I really can't explain how I
turned out to be so pretty.

WHEN OTTO GOT A HOT DOG

When Otto got a hot dog
he stared at it a while,
then dripped a drop of mustard on
and smiled a little smile.

He covered it with relish
which really made him grin,
then spread it thick with mayonnaise
and shoveled onions in.

He splashed it with some ketchup,
as much as he could squeeze,
and tossed on chopped tomatoes
and some shredded cheddar cheese.

He smothered it with sauerkraut,
and bacon bits and beans.
He even added twenty-two
Norwegian canned sardines.

He piled it high with pickles
and peppers by the pound.
He topped it off with chili
then he looked at it and frowned.

He shed a single tiny tear
and gave a little pout,
for Otto hated mustard
so he had to throw it out.

DON'T EVER BITE YOUR SISTER

Don't ever bite your sister.
Don't kick her in the shin.
Don't slap your sister silly
and don't sock her on the chin.

Don't tape a "Kick Me" poster
upon your sister's back.
Don't take your stinky socks off
and then put them in her pack.

Don't purchase plastic spiders
and place them on her head.
Don't leave your rubber rattlesnake
inside your sister's bed.

Don't do this to your sister
for, if you ever do,
I'm pretty sure she may do something
even worse to you.

MY ROBOT DOES MY HOMEWORK

My robot does my homework.
He helps me every night.
The trouble is he doesn't get
too many answers right.

He'd probably do better
at homework but, you see,
I built him, so he only knows
the things he learned from me.

MISTER E.

He only goes by Mister E.
His real name's unknown.
There's no name on his mailbox,
and no number on his phone.

His last name is a question mark.
His first name is a blur.
The photo on his license
is unfocused and obscure.

He always wears disguises
so you'll never see his face.
He'll vanish in a puff of smoke
and leave without a trace.

You'll never have an inkling
of his true identity.
He's a mystifying mystery,
the man called "Mister E."

DON'T BOTHER ANY BUTTERFLIES

Don't bother any butterflies.
Give ladybugs no grief.
Don't irritate the inchworm
as it strolls along the leaf.

Do not besiege the bumblebee
or set upon the fly.
If a spider walks beside you
let the spider sidle by.

Try not to plague the locust.
Let the caterpillar pass.
Investigate no anthill
with your magnifying glass.

Don't terminate the termite
or antagonize the flea.
If a beetle is before you,
let it be, yeah, let it be.

If you should come across a bug
you now know what to do,
for if you do not bug the bug
the bug will not bug you.

A *MELON*CHOLY TALE

Helen Melon fell in love
with little Jerry Berry.
Still, the two were much too young
to run away and marry.

Helen said "We can't elope;
we only met in spring.
Let us wait till autumn.
Then I'll wear your wedding ring.

Through the summer Helen grew;
she gained a lot of weight.
Jerry just grew sweeter
up until their wedding date.

"Honey, do you?" Jerry asked her.
"Yes I do!" she cried.
"Man and wife," declared the preacher.
"You may kiss the bride."

Everyone could plainly see
the pair were so in love.
Jerry looked up to his bride
as she leaned from above.

Just one kiss was all they shared;
now love is her excuse,
why Helen Melon's widowed
and Jerry Berry's juice.

iF i WERE THE PRiNCiPAL

If I were the Principal, boy, things would change.
Our school would be fun, if a little bit strange.
We'd keep kangaroos in the classrooms as pets.
We'd travel to Tonga. We'd learn to fly jets.

We'd get to make movies, and all become stars.
For field trips we'd blast off on rockets to mars.
We'd learn to raise monsters and build time machines.
We'd surf on tsunamis in sleek submarines.

We'd learn to make robots with nuclear brains,
and dig up a dinosaur's fossil remains.
We'd battle with pirates and plunder their gold.
We'd duel with dragons for treasures untold.

We'd practice some potions and magical spells
to stink up the schoolyard with sickening smells,
to make us invisible, eighty feet tall,
or turn into liquid or walk through a wall.

Yes, if I were Principal, that's what we'd do.
We'd lock evil scientists up in the zoo,
while vanquishing villains and capturing crooks.
In other words, we would read many more books.

MY NOSTRIL SMELLS AWESOME

My nostril smells awesome inside of my nose,
a bit like the bloom of a newly picked rose.
It started this morning—I couldn't say why—
and all day it's smelled like banana cream pie.

It has the aroma of freshly baked bread
with hot melted butter and blackberry spread,
and maybe the breeze of a warm afternoon
that follows a thunderstorm early in June.

It smells like a pine forest, right by a lake,
and chocolate chip cookies my mom likes to bake,
like kettle corn pop-popping over a fire,
and laundry, the moment it's out of the dryer.

My nostril smells awesome, so I have a plan
to sit and enjoy it as long as I can.
Don't ask how it happened; I really can't say.
Perhaps it's my finger that's smelling this way.

MY PUPPY PUNCHED ME IN THE EYE

My puppy punched me in the eye.
My rabbit whacked my ear.
My ferret gave a frightful cry
and roundhouse kicked my rear.

My lizard flipped me upside down.
My kitten kicked my head.
My hamster slammed me to the ground
and left me nearly dead.

So my advice? Avoid regrets;
no matter what you do,
don't ever let the family pets
take lessons in kung fu.

BLUEBEARD AND REDBEARD AND BLACKBEARD

Bluebeard and Redbeard and Blackbeard, they say,
hijacked a ship and went sailing away.
Seaward they scudded and skipped on the breeze,
searching for treasure to plunder and seize.

Riches, regrettably, couldn't be found.
Ships bearing booty were nowhere around.
Therefore the buccaneers wandered afloat
thinking of things they could do with their boat.

Bluebeard said, "Aargh, since we've nothing to do,
why don't we paint our new pirate ship blue?"
Redbeard spoke up, saying, "Aye, but instead,
wouldn't ye rather we painted her red?"

Blackbeard said, "Blimey, you're both off the track.
No other color's as handsome as black."
"Blue!" shouted Bluebeard, and Redbeard yelled "Red!"
Blackbeard said, "Black! You're both cracked in the head!"

Redbeard grabbed brushes and buckets and paints
over his shipmate's insistent complaints.
Rather than letting him paint the ship red,
they got some blue paint and black paint instead.

Swiftly the three of them painted their boat,
each a completely dissimilar coat,
making a color not red, black, or blue;
mixing, instead, an entirely new hue.

That was the last that was seen of the three
simply because they refused to agree.
They weren't torpedoed or shelled or harpooned.
They disappeared, for their ship was marooned.

MY FOOT FELL ASLEEP

My foot fell asleep
right inside of my shoe
from sitting around
having nothing to do.
It hadn't drank warm milk
nor tried to count sheep;
it just wasn't busy,
and fell right asleep.

You see, in my shoe
it gets lonely and boring,
which made my foot sleepy,
and soon it was snoring.
My foot snored so loudly
my shoe began flapping.
My foot didn't notice—
it kept right on napping!

ZZZZZ

It slept through the morning
and most of the day,
despite that my other foot
wanted to play.
It took a siesta.
It slumbered inert.
It nodded through dinner.
It dozed through dessert.

I'm now in my bed
and I've been up all night.
I'm trying to sleep,
although, try as I might,
my foot slept all day
(what a foolish mistake!)
now I can't fall asleep
'cause my foot's wide awake!

I'M A WIZARD, I'M A WARLOCK

I'm a wizard, I'm a warlock,
I'm a wonder of the age.
I'm a sorcerer, magician,
prestidigitator, mage.

I can change into a chicken,
or perhaps a purple pig.
I can wave my wand and, presto,
I'm a waffle with a wig.

With the power in my pinky
I can burst like a balloon
or transform into a tiger
with the head of a baboon.

If I wiggle on my earlobe
or I knock upon my knee,
I become a dancing doughnut
or a turtle in a tree.

Just a simple incantation
and I deftly disappear,
which I never should have done
because I've been this way all year.

And despite my mighty magic
I'm impossible to see,
for I never learned the spells I need
to turn back into me.

CHICKEN POX CONNECT-THE-DOTS

I had a case of chicken pox.
My skin was strewn with spots.
And so I grabbed a marker
and I played connect-the-dots.

I started on my pinky toes.
The lines went up my feet,
around my ankles, shins, and knees,
and right across on my seat.

They circled 'round my belly button,
outward toward my hips,
then up my chest, around my neck,
and past my chin and lips.

The lines continued on my ears,
my eyebrows, cheeks, and nose,
then out my arms and in again
and downward to my toes.

I ran and got a mirror,
and I smiled as I was seeing
by linking all the dots
I'd drawn a 3-D human being.

WHEN VEGETABLES ARE ANGRY

When vegetables are angry
does it mean they're in a stew?
When morning says good morning
does it ask how do you dew?

When mountaintops are spying
would you say they're sneaking peeks?
When water spills on onions
does it turn them into leeks?

To be a good conductor
do you really have to train?
If Superman retired
would he live on Lois Lane?

If streets required clothing
would you buy your street a dress?
If restaurants were dirty
would you eat inside the mess?

Whenever you're impatient
does it mean you're losing wait?
If six bought lunch for seven
would you care how much he ate?

When cheese pots say good evening
do they bid a fond adieu?
When vegetables are angry
does it mean they're in a stew?

WALLY WARDS THE SWORD SWALLOWER

Wally Wards
swallowed swords,
daggers, dirks,
and razor blades,
lances, spears,
garden shears,
sabers, scissors,
spikes, and spades.

Wally's jaws
welcomed saws,
hatchets, axes,
power drills,
arrows, picks,
sharpened sticks;
that's how Wally
got his thrills.

All the same
it's a shame
Wally Wards
should lose his life.
Wally croaked
when he choked
on a plastic
butter knife.

MiRROR, MiRROR

Mirror, mirror, by the sink,
tell me what you truly think.
Am I fat or am I thin?
Will I lose or should I win?

Am I short? Perhaps too tall?
Are my ears a bit too small?
Is my nose exactly right?
Do I have an overbite?

Am I weak or super strong?
Is my hair too short or long?
Am I smart or rather dumb?
Can you say what I'll become?

Am I nerdy? Am I cool?
Am I awful? Do I rule?
Am I great or do I stink?
Mirror, mirror by the sink.

LEARNING HOW TO JUGGLE

I've been learning how to juggle
with facility and flair.
I'm attempting keeping
six or seven beanbags in the air.

I'll propel some pears and peaches
and assorted other fruit.
I'll toss apricots and apples
as I practice my pursuit.

I will demonstrate my nimbleness
and knack for pitching pegs
with bananas, bats, and bowling balls,
and eighty-seven eggs.

Then with fifty flaming torches
I'll inspire the crowds to awe.
I will heave a hundred hammers,
hurl a hatchet and a saw.

You'll be spellbound and astonished
as I sling and try to snatch,
for I'm excellent at throwing.
(I just haven't learned to catch.)

MY MAGIC HAT iS MARVELOUS

My magic hat is marvelous.
It's round and rather red.
It looks just like a baseball cap
and sits atop my head.

The things it does are magical;
it helps to keep me warm,
and keeps my hair from getting wet
whenever there's a storm.

It's magic how it shades my eyes
and holds my hair in place.
And if I wear it backwards,
it reveals my smiling face.

It's magically adjustable;
just pull the little strap.
And yet, it looks exactly
like a normal baseball cap.

Its powers are mysterious.
You simply have to see.
I'll gladly let you look
for just a twenty-dollar fee.

i BOUGHT A PET BANANA

I bought a pet banana
and I tried to teach him tricks,
but he wasn't any good at
catching balls or fetching sticks.

He could never catch a Frisbee,
and he wouldn't sit or speak,
though we practiced every afternoon
and evening for a week.

He refused to shake or wave or crawl
or beg or take a bow,
and I tried, but couldn't make him bark
or get him to meow.

He was terrible at playing dead.
He couldn't jump a rope.
When he wouldn't do a single trick
I simply gave up hope.

Though I liked my pet banana,
I returned him with regret.
Boy, I sure do hope this watermelon
makes a better pet.

CAN'T SLEEP

I'm battling insomnia.
I cannot get to sleep
despite a rather valiant
attempt at counting sheep.

I counted to a hundred.
Then I had a glass of milk.
I fluffed my little pillow
in its pillowcase of silk.

I made a pot of herbal tea
and drank at least a cup.
I sang myself a lullaby
and pulled my blankie up.

I plugged my ears with cotton balls.
I covered up my eyes.
I took relaxing breaths
and did a stretching exercise.

I've tried and tried to get to sleep
but just can't find a way.
It's looking like I'll have to
stay awake in class today.

SLEEPING BEAUTY

Sleeping Beauty pricked her thumb,
started feeling overcome.
Probably she would have died
as the witch had prophesied,
but the fairies had her blessed
so she just got beauty rest.
For a hundred fifty years
she missed balls and film premieres
till Prince Charming came along
singing out a cheerful song.
Kneeling down he kissed her cheek
hoping that she'd wake and speak.
Sleeping Beauty raised an arm
reaching for the snooze alarm
and her waking words were these:
"Just need five more minutes please."

MY UNCLE HAD AN ANT FARM

My uncle had an ant farm
where he raised a lot of ants.
He taught a few to play guitar;
he taught a few to dance.

Another one, or maybe two,
he tutored on the ant kazoo.
He bought them little xylophones,
and teeny-tiny slide trombones,
submicroscopic saxophones,
and itsy-bitsy baritones.
He trained a few to beat a drum,
and all the rest learned how to hum,
until, at last, they had a band
parading in the ant farm sand.

And yet no matter where you stood,
or where you put your ear,
those little ants were much too small
for anyone to hear.

MY ELEPHANT THiNKS i'M WONDERFUL

My elephant thinks I'm wonderful.
My elephant thinks I'm cool.
My elephant hangs around with me
and follows me off to school.

My elephant likes the way I look.
He thinks that I'm fun and smart.
He thinks that I'm kind and generous
and have a terrific heart.

My elephant thinks I'm brave and bold.
He's proud of my strength and guts.
But mostly he likes the way I smell.
My elephant thinks I'm nuts.

SNIFF SNIFF

80

LEFTY THE LiFTER

Tonight I write of Lefty Wright,
a lifter slightly gifted,
who nightly lifted left and right
so deftly all he lifted.

Lefty lifted, on his left,
aloft a hefty crate.
Lefty lifted, on his right,
a slightly lighter weight.

So though Lefty lifted deftly,
shifting as he lifted,
Lefty, listing swiftly leftly,
drifted off a cliff did.

Rites were read for Lefty Wright
to Wrights he left bereft.
Despite his might, from quite a height,
yes, Lefty Wright has left.

THE TIGER AND THE ZEBRA

The tiger phoned the zebra
and invited him to dine.
He said, "If you could join me
that would simply be divine."
The zebra said, "I thank you,
but respectfully decline.
I heard you ate the antelope;
he was a friend of mine."

On hearing this the tiger cried,
"I must admit it's true!
I also ate the buffalo,
the llama and the gnu.
And, yes, I ate the warthog,
the gazelle and kangaroo,
but I could never eat a creature
beautiful as you.

"You see I have a secret
I'm embarrassed to confide:
I look on you with envy
and a modicum of pride.
Of all the creatures ever known,"
the tiger gently sighed,
"it seems we are the only two
with such a stripy hide.

"Now seeing how we share this
strong resemblance of the skin,
I only can conclude that we are
just as close as kin.
This means you are my brother
and, though fearsome I have been,
I could not eat my brother,
that would surely be a sin."

The zebra thought, and then replied,
"I'm certain you are right.
The stripy coats we both possess
are such a handsome sight!
My brother, will you let me
reconsider if I might?
My calendar is empty so
please let us dine tonight."

The tiger met the zebra in
his brand-new fancy car
and drove him to a restaurant
which wasn't very far.
And when they both were seated
at a table near the bar,
the zebra asked, "What's on the grill?"
The tiger said, "You are."

"But please, you cannot dine on me!"
the outraged zebra cried.
"To cook me up and eat me
is a thing I can't abide.
You asked me for your trust
and I unwarily complied.
You said you could not eat me.
Now you plan to have me fried?"

"And what about the envy
and the modicum of pride?
And what of us as brothers
since we share a stripy hide?"
"I'm sorry," said the tiger
and he smiled as he replied,
"but I love the taste of zebra
so, in other words, I lied."

MY FROG HAS GOT A STEERING WHEEL

My frog has got a steering wheel,
a radio, a door,
a hefty V-8 engine,
and a stick shift on the floor.

My frog is a convertible
with comfy leather seats.
I drive my frog to go to work
or cruise around the streets.

But now my frog is missing.
Though parked it on the road,
I didn't plug the meter
and it must have gotten toad.

i OFTEN CONTRADiCT MYSELF

I often contradict myself.
Oh no, I never do.
I argue with me day and night.
That simply isn't true.

Oh yes it is. Oh no it's not.
I do this all day long.
Oh no I don't. Oh yes I do.
That's right. No way! It's wrong.

I'm really quite agreeable.
I argue night and day.
I love to be around myself.
I wish I'd go away.

So if you see me arguing,
it's certain that you won't.
I like to contradict myself.
I promise you I don't.

TERRIBLE DREAM

I'm feeling rather ragged.
I'm feeling rather rough.
I'm looking like I stayed up late,
and didn't sleep enough.

I went to sleep at bedtime
and dreamt all through the night,
but when I woke this morning
I was feeling far from right.

For though I drifted quickly,
and slumbered long and deep,
I'm totally exhausted!
See, I dreamed I couldn't sleep.

i CLONED MYSELF ON FRiDAY NiGHT

I cloned myself on Friday night.
By Saturday at three
my clone had made another clone.
They both looked just like me.

They walked like me and talked like me
and acted like me too.
They wore my clothes and used my stuff
and did the things I do.

But worst of all they made more clones
who then made even more,
and soon my house was overrun
and I was getting sore.

They wouldn't do my laundry,
clean my room, or make my bed.
They wouldn't wash the dishes
or do anything I said.

Instead they sat and watched TV
and played computer games.
They ate up all my favorite snacks
and called each other names.

And now they like to stay up late
and keep me wide awake.
My life is wrecked but, still, I hope
you'll learn from my mistake.

Don't ever try to clone yourself.
But, if you ever do,
you'd better hope your clones are not
exactly just like you.

MOVING TO CHINA

I'm moving to China as soon as I can.
Or maybe Jamaica or maybe Japan.
I'm heading for someplace a long way away,
so try all you want, but you can't make me stay.

You won't see my face around here anymore.
I'm practically ready to walk out the door.
I'm taking my stuff and beginning to pack.
I'm leaving forever and not coming back.

I really don't care if I travel by train,
or sailboat, or steamship, or snowplow, or plane,
or surfboard, or bulldozer, bobsled, or bike,
or truck, or toboggan, or tractor, or trike.

As long as I end up a long way from here,
in Norway, New Zealand, Nepal, or Zaire,
or Pakistan, Poland perhaps, or Peru,
or Turkey, or Thailand, or, yes, Timbuktu.

I hope that you don't think I'm selfish or rude.
It's just that I haven't got money or food.
I promise—you'll see—I'll be gone in a flash,
as soon as you feed me and lend me some cash.

OUR TEACHER'S LIKE NO OTHER TEACHER

Our teacher's like no other teacher we've seen.
She likes to wear costumes from last Halloween.
While shouting a sonnet she'll dance with a broom,
then sprinkle confetti all over the room.

She asks the opinions of Mr. Levesque,
the mannequin head that she keeps on her desk.
She jokes with the hamster and claims he can talk.
She wrestles erasers and argues with chalk.

She likes to make sculptures from typewriter parts
and bakes us her heavenly blackberry tarts.
For homework, she says that we have to go play,
and watch no TV for the rest of the day.

Our teacher is either completely insane
or some kind of genius with oodles of brain.
But whether it's madness or cerebral powers,
we don't think it matters; we're glad that she's ours.

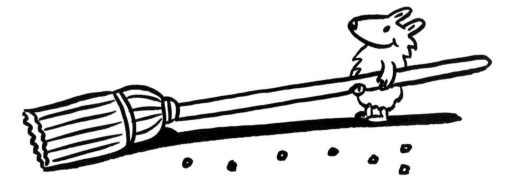

MELODY RING

Melody Ring has a musical family.
A musical family has Melody Ring.
Her mother likes opera and symphony music,
and frequently joins in a chorus to sing.

But Melody Ring doesn't know how to sing.
She's unable to utter a hum or a chirp.
She opens her mouth with the best of intentions
but all she can manage to make is a "BURRRP!"

Her father is partial to country and western.
He plays his harmonica all through the day,
then strums on his banjo or pounds the piano;
there's hardly an instrument her father can't play.

But Melody Ring doesn't play any instruments;
not an accordion, trumpet or flute.
She'll pick up a piccolo planning to play
but before she can blow it, she'll let out a "TOOOOT!"

Her brother plays drums and electric guitar
and he jams with his friends in a rock-and-roll band.
He also spins turntables, scratching and rapping,
and loves to play music his parents can't stand.

But Melody isn't as cool as her brother.
She can't spin a record. She can't even rap.
She picks up the microphone, ready to rock,
but the best she can do is a "PHHHHHT" and a "BRAAAAP!"

Melody's parents are truly embarrassed.
They simply don't know what to say or to do.
And so they've decided to not say a word...
at least until next year, when Melody's two.

HOORAY! HOORAY! IT'S NEW YEAR'S DAY!

Hooray! Hooray! It's New Year's Day!
The day we start anew.
So this year I've decided
to become a kangaroo.

Or maybe I will learn to fly,
or how to walk through walls,
or how to turn invisible,
or surf on waterfalls.

I'll make myself elastic
and I'll teach myself to shrink.
I'll turn into a liquid
and I'll pour me down the sink.

I'll visit other planets
and meet aliens galore.
I'll travel to the distant past
and ride a dinosaur.

I've got so many wondrous plans.
I'm starting right away.
Yes, this will be the best year yet.
Hooray! It's New Year's Day!

A STRANGE OLD MAN FELL OUT OF BED

A strange old man fell out of bed
and hit the floor and bonked his head.
It bonked so hard, to his dismay,
his head fell off and rolled away.
And when he found he'd lost his head
and realized he must be dead,
he fell back into bed and then
he bonked his head back on again.

MELINDA MCKNIGHT

Melinda McKnight is extremely polite,
but only on Sundays at seven fifteen.
On Mondays at one she will argue for fun.
On Tuesdays at two she's completely obscene.

On Wednesdays at nine she will grumble and whine.
She'll croak and complain if she can't have her way.
On Thursdays at three she's as rude as can be.
She'll fuss and throw fits for the rest of the day.

On Fridays at four she will slam every door.
She'll screech and she'll squabble on Saturday night.
And Sundays she's mean until seven fifteen
when Melinda McKnight is extremely polite.

MY PENGUIN

My penguin looks quite dashing
in his top hat, coat, and tails,
with a cummerbund from Macy's
and a tie from Bloomingdales.

My penguin likes to party
in his dapper black tuxedo,
but whenever he goes swimming
he wears nothing but his Speedo.

TODAY i DECiDED TO MAKE UP A WORD

Today I decided to make up a word,
like flonk, or scrandana, or hankly, or smurred.
My word will be useful and sound really cool;
a word like chindango, or fraskle, or spewl.

My friends and my teachers will all be impressed
to learn that I've made up a word like extrest,
or crondic, or crambly, or squantion, or squank.
Whenever they use it, it's me that they'll thank.

They'll call me a genius and give me a prize,
repeating my word, be it shimble, or glize,
or frustice, or frongry, or frastamazoo,
or pandaverandamalandamaloo.

You'll see it on TV shows one of these days.
They'll use it in movies. They'll put it in plays.
They'll shout it from rooftops! The headlines will read,
"This Kid Has Invented the Word that We Need!"

I'll make up my word, and I'll share it with you,
and you can tell people from here to Peru;
the old ones, the young ones, and those in between...
as soon as I figure out what it should mean.

i DREAMED THAT i WAS SOUND ASLEEP

I dreamed that I was sound asleep
and lying in my bed,
and in my dream another dream
was drifting through my head.

And in that dream I had a dream
and in it I was dreaming
a dream about a dream until
I woke up nearly screaming.

It seems to dream you're dreaming
is a terrible mistake.
I can't tell which dream ended
and I'm not sure I'm awake.

SEA MONSTER'S COMPLAINT

My breakfast never varies;
it's the same thing every day.
And lunch and dinner likewise
make me yawn and turn away.

I'm craving something different.
I'm in need of something new.
Some pickles, some lasagna,
and a chocolate cake or two.

I'd like a dozen pizzas
and some carryout Chinese,
a turkey, ham, and pot roast,
with potatoes, pies, and peas.

I want a bag of burgers,
and a barrelful of rice.
I'll wash it down with twenty quarts
of soda pop on ice.

My taste buds need variety
to pass between my lips.
No more of just the same old thing!
I'm sick of fish and ships.

ANDY HANDY'S HARDWARE STORE

Andy Handy's hardware store
sells things that no one needs;
a doorknob for a doghouse door,
a kit for growing weeds,

storage bins for storing air,
a hook for holding hooks,
a key that opens locks of hair,
a battery for books,

garbage for your garbage pails,
a wrench for cracking nuts,
a hammer for your fingernails,
a saw for paper cuts,

drills for drilling holes in socks,
and tulip bulbs for lamps,
extension cords for broken clocks,
a clamp for clamping clamps,

glue for plugging showerheads,
and paint for painting drapes,
a mower for your flower beds,
some tape for taping tapes,

packs of poison ivy seeds,
you'll find all this and more,
yes, everything you'll never need's
at Handy's Hardware Store.

WHILE STROLLING DOWN THE BEACH TODAY

While strolling down the beach today
I came upon a lamp.
It was dusty, it was dirty,
it was dingy, it was damp.

It appeared that all it needed
to restore it was a scrub,
so I dug it from the salty sand
and gave a little rub.

In a moment it was glistening.
Then, right before my eyes
there appeared a purple genie
of incalculable size.

He was massive and magnificent
and glorious and grand,
and he bowed and said dramatically,
"Your wish is my command."

It was then I did the stupid thing
I now regret I did,
for I know I'll never be again
an ordinary kid.

I considered just a moment,
then I looked him in the eye
and I asked that giant genie,
"Would you please make me a pie?"

PETER PRIM THE FIRE-EATER

Peter Prim the fire-eater
ate a propane camping heater,
followed by a butane lighter,
and a barbecue igniter.
Next he drank some gasoline,
and a quart of kerosene
(or perhaps it was a liter;
no one knows for sure but Peter).
Last, to finish off the batch
Peter ate a flaming match.
Bits of Peter Prim, they say,
lit a half a mile away
(or perhaps a kilometer;
who's to say except for Peter?).
Nothing more was seen of him.
Rest in pieces, Peter Prim.

i BOUGHT A MASERATi

I bought a Maserati
and a new Mercedes-Benz,
plus a brand new Lamborghini
I could show off to my friends.

I purchased a Ferrari
and an Aston Martin too,
and a Porsche and a Jaguar
and a BMW.

I had them all delivered
to my mansion in the hills.
I like to sit and look at them,
imagining the thrills.

For though it's fun to be
the richest nine-year-old alive,
I'm sure I'll like it better
when I'm old enough to drive.

PET SHOPPING

While shopping at the pet store
I got my fondest wish.
I bought myself a fish bowl
and then a pair of fish.

And since I was already
out shopping at the store
I thought I ought to purchase
another smidgen more.

And so I got a rabbit,
a hamster and a frog,
a gerbil and a turtle,
a parrot and a dog.

I purchased an iguana,
a tortoise and a rat,
an eight-foot anaconda,
a monkey and a cat.

A guinea pig, a gecko,
a ferret and a mouse,
and had them all delivered,
directly to my house.

My sister went berzerko!
She's now installing locks,
because I said her bedroom
would be their litter box!

MY GOLDFISH TOOK UP TENNIS

My goldfish took up tennis.
They installed a little net
at the bottom of their fish tank
for their first official set.

They got tennis balls and racquets.
They got tennis shoes and shorts,
for my fish are fond of tennis
more than any other sports.

It's a funny thing to watch them
when they practice every day,
as they serve and watch their tennis balls
just up and float away.

THE FiSHERMAN AND HiS WiFE

Once upon a time there was
a man who caught a fish
that begged to be released
and in exchange would grant a wish.

"A talking fish?" the man exclaimed,
"Of course I'll set you free!
And in return I hope you'll
grant this single wish for me."

The man went home and told his wife
he'd caught a talking fish,
explaining how he'd let it go
and got his fondest wish.

He said, "I got the one thing
that I've wanted all my life."
She asked him, "What?" And he replied,
"I wished I had a wife."

YOU CAN NEVER BE TOO CAREFUL

You can never be too careful.
That's what I always say,
and so I wear a hat, or two,
in case my hair turns gray.
I've thirteen tires on my car,
in case I get a flat.
I wear my pants size fifty-three,
in case I grow too fat.

You can never be too careful.
I'm sure you'll find it's true.
I see the doctor every day,
in case I catch the flu.
I carry twenty handkerchiefs,
in case I have to sneeze,
and forty-seven bandages,
in case I skin my knees.

You can never be too careful,
so if I take a walk,
I tiptoe everywhere I go
and whisper when I talk.
I hide my money in a box,
and lock it up inside Fort Knox.
My house is made of bricks and rocks.
The front door has a hundred locks.

But now I have a problem, see,
I'm locked inside without the key.
I've lost it and I can't get free.
I hid it much too carefully!

I ONLY WANT KETCHUP

I only want ketchup.
It's all that I like.
I don't need a burger.
I don't need a bike.

I don't want a tuba,
a truck or a train,
bananas, bandanas,
pianos or rain.

I'll pass on canasta,
gymnastics and chess.
I don't need a diamond
a dog or a dress.

I'm fine without fairies,
canaries or figs,
tomatoes, tornadoes,
tortillas and twigs.

I'd give up guitars
and carnations and cheese,
the stars in the sky
and the wind in the trees.

I don't need a hug
or an afternoon hike.
Just pass me the ketchup.
It's all that I like.

THE MONSTERS' MUSICAL CONTEST

When the musical contest for monsters convened,
the Wolfman was howling and played like a fiend.
Then Dracula jammed, but flew into a rage
when Frankenstein's torch singing lit up the stage.

The Mummy, he rapped with the aid of a band,
but stopped when The Blob ate his microphone stand.
The Blob, by the way, also swallowed The Fly.
(I don't know why he swallowed The Fly.)

The Creature that came from that famous lagoon
was booed by the ghosts when he sang out of tune.
Dr. Jekyll had stage fright and ran off to hide,
while Igor sang love songs to Frankenstein's Bride.

The Thing did impressions. The Boogeyman danced.
The Zombie just stood there, completely entranced.
The Invisible Man played his air guitar well,
but no one could see him so no one could tell.

They played through the night having oodles of fun,
but couldn't determine which monster had won.
And so they decided they'd have to convene
and do it again on the next Halloween.

MEAT LOAF

My mother made a meat loaf
but I think she made it wrong.
It could be that she cooked it
just a little bit too long.

She pulled it from the oven;
and we all began to choke.
The meat loaf was on fire
and the kitchen filled with smoke.

The smoke detectors squealed
from all the flaming meat loaf haze.
My father used his drink
to try extinguishing the blaze.

Mom shrieked and dropped the meat loaf;
it exploded with a boom,
and splattered blackened globs on
every surface in the room.

The dog passed out. The kitten hid.
My brother screamed and fled.
The baby ate a piece of meat loaf
sticking to her head.

My father started yelling
and my sister went berserk.
But I kept cool and said, "At least
our smoke detectors work."

IGNORE THE RED RHINOCEROS

Ignore the red rhinoceros.
Forget he's even there.
Pretend you cannot see him
wave his pom-poms in the air.

Dismiss his purple tutu
and his orange leotard.
If he begins to bossa nova,
pay him no regard.

Do not be disconcerted
by his color or his size,
and if he starts to shimmy
try to stifle your surprise.

Pay simply no attention
to that disco-dancing beast.
Just act as if you find him
not distracting in the least.

Though now and then he startles me
and sometimes makes me squirm,
I've practically forgotten
this peculiar pachyderm.

So try to do as I do:
think of something else instead.
Ignore the red rhinoceros
that's dancing on my head.

MR. INVISIBLE

Mr. Invisible doesn't wear clothes,
ensuring he'll never be seen.
He'll sneak in a restaurant, and slip in the back
to sample their tasty cuisine.

Mr. Invisible likes to read books,
so he slides through the library doors.
He visits museums, he hangs out in parks,
he saunters through churches and stores.

He dances down alleyways, rambles on roads,
meanders in plazas and malls.
He bounds over bridges, he skips around squares,
he tiptoes through tunnels and halls.

Mr. Invisible strides up the street
quite certain he'll never be caught.
But Mr. Invisible ought to wear clothes,
because Mr. Invisible's not.

SOMETHING i NEED TO REMEMBER

There's something I need to remember,
but somehow it seems I forgot.
I'll sit here until I recall it.
I won't move an inch from this spot.

Is sleeping the thing I've forgotten?
Did I not remember to eat?
Did I take a shower this morning?
Is all of my homework complete?

Should I be at home or at school?
Or watching a show on TV?
Are some of my friends coming over?
Is anyone waiting for me?

And why am I sitting here thinking,
not moving an inch from this spot?
I'm sure that there must be a reason,
but somehow it seems I forgot.

RAPUNZEL! RAPUNZEL!

"Rapunzel! Rapunzel! You've cut off your hair!
Your billowing tresses are no longer there.
That mohawk you're sporting is spiky and pink.
I'm really not certain just what I should think.

"I came here expecting to clamber a braid,
ascending your tower to come to your aid.
Instead, I have suffered the greatest of shocks
to find that you've cut off your lovely blonde locks."

"Prince Charming, Prince Charming," Rapunzel replied,
"I have no intention of being your bride.
We will not get married. We will not elope.
I've cut off my hair and I've braided a rope.

"You came here to visit me once every day,
and promised that soon you would take me away,
but you were too clueless to even conceive
of cutting my hair off so we could just leave.

"I cannot believe you were such a big dope.
I come and I go as I please with my rope.
And so, I'm afraid I can't give you my hand,
in spite of the fabulous wedding you planned."

From then on Rapunzel was known through the land.
She toured the world in a rock-and-roll band.
And silly Prince Charming, with rocks in his head,
rode off and got married to Snow White instead.

TODAY i HAD A PROBLEM

Today I had a problem
when I tried to make my bed.
My blankets and my comforter
got wrapped around my head.

I went to fluff the pillows
but the pillow cover tore,
and feathers flew all over
as I stumbled 'round the floor.

I accidentally grabbed the sheets
and pulled them as I fell.
I have to say, it seems
my day's not starting off too well.

I tripped upon a pillowcase
and landed in a heap.
Good grief! That's it! I'm staying here
and going back to sleep!

THIS POEM'S NOT ABOUT A DOG

This poem's not about a dog.
It's not about a cat.
It's not about a fish or frog
or anything like that.

It's also not about my shoe,
or cows from outer space,
or purple pigs from Timbuktu,
or weasels on your face.

This poem's not the slightest bit
about some guy named Fred.
There are no robot ducks in it,
or hippos overhead.

It's not about electric sheep,
or eighty-five times nine,
or watching grandpa fall asleep,
or cheese from Lichtenstein.

It's not about a hungry hog
who ate a bowling ball.
This poem's not about a dog,
or anything at all.

CHESTER SYLVESTER THE JESTER

I'm Chester Sylvester the Jester.
I strike a peculiar pose.
I dress up in plaid polyester
with pens sticking out of my nose.

My hat is a live armadillo.
My pockets are brimming with cheese.
I chew on a camel-hair pillow
and swing from a flying trapeze.

I often wear spandex pajamas
with paisley and polka-dot socks,
and bleat like a roomful of llamas
while sticking my head in a box.

I cover myself in confetti,
with mayonnaise poured in my hair,
then stand on my head in spaghetti
while waving my hands in the air.

I've studied my skill all semester.
I'm utterly crazed and berserk.
I'm Chester Sylvester the Jester;
please help me... I'm looking for work.

FLOWER GiRL

Sarah Sears, to whoops and cheers,
grew petunias from her ears.
Then, with grace and savoir faire,
sprouted tulips from her hair.
Next she smiled and struck a pose;
orchids blossomed from her nose,
and with unexpected skill,
she produced a daffodil.
Peonies and prairie rockets
germinated from her pockets.
Poppies bloomed between her toes.
Pansies covered all her clothes.
This went on for hours and hours,
blooming petals, budding flowers,
till her parents came and got her,
taking home their floral daughter,
where, with tears upon her face,
she threw out her empty vase.
Sarah sniffed and blew her nose;
all she wanted was a rose.

MR. MEECHER, SCiENCE TEACHER

Mr. Meecher, science teacher,
made a complicated creature,
like a science fiction feature,
in the classroom yesterday.
It was such a weird creation,
this fantastic formulation
was a magical mutation
that could undulate and sway.

It would wobble, it would wiggle.
It would jostle, it would jiggle,
making all the students giggle
as it bopped and bounced around.
It was stumbling and unstable.
Mr. Meecher was unable
to control it on the table,
and it tumbled to the ground.

It was jamming, it was jumping.
It was boogieing and bumping.
It was thundering and thumping,
like a disco dancing blob.
Mr. Meecher tried to grab it,
but he couldn't seem to nab it;
it would scramble like a rabbit.
It would duck and weave and bob.

So he gave the thing a kick. It
then became a sticky wicket.
It was tricky, it was quick; it
promptly tackled him instead.
Now you know why Mr. Meecher,
our intrepid science teacher,
has a complicated creature
disco dancing on his head.

i'M ONLY HALF A WEREWOLF

I was bitten by a werewolf
with a weak, halfhearted bite,
and became a half a werewolf;
on my left, but not my right.

So now when the moon is halfway full,
my face grows halfway hairy.
And my left-hand claws and single fang
are surely semi-scary.

Now I nearly need to stay up late.
I partly want to prowl.
I've been feeling fairly frisky.
I have half a mind to howl.

If you ever see me coming
you should turn and run away,
for the odds are fifty-fifty
you'll regret it if you stay.

Yes, I may be half a werewolf,
with my fleas and doggy breath,
but I promise, if we ever meet,
I'll scare you half to death.

POOR CINDERELLA

Poor Cinderella, whose stepmom was mean,
could never see films rated PG-13.
She hadn't a cell phone and no DVD,
no notebook computer or pocket TV.
She wasn't allowed to play video games.
The tags on her clothes had unfashionable names.
Her shoes were not trendy enough to be cool.
No limousine chauffeur would drive her to school.
Her house had no drawing room; only a den.
Her bedtime, poor darling, was quarter past ten!

Well one day Prince Charming declared that a ball
would be held in his honor and maidens from all
over the kingdom were welcome to come
and party to techno and jungle house drum.

But Poor Cinderella, with nothing to wear,
collapsed in her stepmother's La-Z-Boy chair.
She let out a sigh, with a lump in her throat,
then sniffled and picked up the TV remote.
She surfed channel zero to channel one-ten
then went back to zero and started again.
She watched music videos, sitcoms and sports,
commercials and talk shows and weather reports.

But no fairy godmother came to her side
to offer a dress or a carriage to ride.
So Poor Cinderella's been sitting there since,
while one of her stepsisters married the Prince.
She sits there and sadly complains to the screen,
if only her stepmother wasn't so mean.

ON PiCTURE DAY i WORE A SUiT

On picture day I wore a suit.
My teacher told me I'd look cute.
I wonder why she got so mad.
I wore the only one I had.

i BUiLT MYSELF A TiME MACHiNE

I built myself a time machine
tomorrow afternoon,
then traveled back to yesterday,
and very, very soon
I'll re-create my time machine
and travel once again
to yesterday where, like before,
I'll wait two days and then
I'll build myself a time machine.
I'm such a nincompoop.
I never should have made this thing.
I'm stuck inside a loop.

JUAN AND TU

Juan ran races.
Tu ran too.
Tu won one and
Juan won two.

Hugh ran one with
Juan and Tu.
Hugh won none when
he ran too.

Who won two when
Tu won one?
Juan won two and
Hugh won none.

i WROTE MYSELF A LETTER

I wrote myself a letter.
I mailed it right away.
And, sure enough, the carrier
delivered it today.

I couldn't wait to get it.
I nearly had to shout.
I quickly tore the envelope
and pulled the letter out.

I anxiously unfolded it
but now I must concede,
I'm clueless as to what it says.
I haven't learned to read.

MY CAR IS CONSTRUCTED OF PICKLES

My car is constructed of pickles.
It's wonderfully crunchy and sweet.
If ever I'm hungry while driving
I pull off a pickle to eat.

The engine is made out of gherkins.
The dashboard's an extra-large dill.
The windows and wipers are kosher
as well as the bumpers and grille.

The hood's made of hamburger slices.
The gas tank is brimming with brine.
The doors are delectably salty.
The stick shift is simply divine.

There's one little problem I'm having.
I'm sure you would know what I mean
if ever you saw this contraption;
my marvelous pickle machine.

I guess I've included my auto
in just a few too many meals
and now it won't budge when I start it;
I shouldn't have eaten the wheels.

GLADIOLA'S GARDEN

Gladiola's garden grows
not a radish nor a rose.
Not a pansy, peach or pear.
No azaleas anywhere.

Not a pumpkin, parsnip, plum,
carrot or chrysanthemum.
No forget-me-not or fig.
Not a single sprout or twig.

No carnations, cabbage, corn.
Not a thistle, thatch, or thorn.
Not a berry. Not a bean.
Nothing yet remotely green.

Watering and sprinkling seeds,
watching warily for weeds,
Gladiola rakes and hoes,
yet her garden never grows.

Still, she doesn't seem to mind.
That's the way it was designed.
Gladiola's quite content
gardening upon cement.

I'M BUILDING A ROCKET

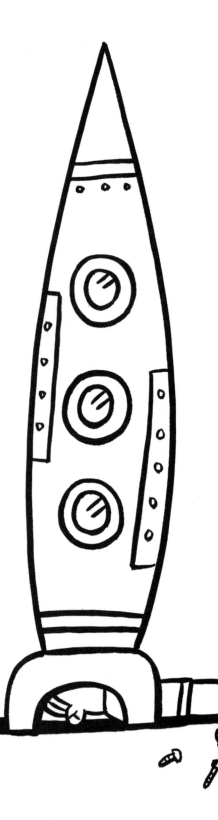

I'm building a rocket.
As soon as I'm done
I'm taking my friends
on a trip to the sun.

But what do you mean
that the sun is too hot?
Oh well, I suppose
I'll just pick a new spot.

I'm building a rocket.
I'm finishing soon
and taking my friends
on a trip to the moon!

But what do you mean
that the moon has no air?
Well dang, then I guess
that we can't go up there.

I'm building a rocket.
It's going to fly.
I'm taking my friends
way up high in the sky.

But what do you mean
when you ask how we'll land?
This rocket is harder
to build than I planned.

To heck with the rocket.
It's out in the shed.
My friends can take me out
for pizza instead.

ANNA GRAHAM

Silly, mixed-up Anna Graham
often mixes up her words.
She says calm instead of clam.
Shred will sometimes come out herds.

Notes are stone and news is sewn.
Bakers, breaks, and aches are chase.
Iron beat is baritone.
Cape routes just means outer space.

Geraldine is realigned.
Mites are times, and limes are smile.
Denim often comes out mined.
Relatives are versatile.

Steak is skate and tale is late.
Name is mispronounced as mean.
Breathe in turns to hibernate.
Bargained sounds like gabardine.

Pore is rope and poles are slope.
Mash is sham and balm is lamb.
Poem always makes her mope;
silly, mixed-up Anna Graham.

MY DOG LIKES TO DISCO

My doggy likes to disco dance.
He boogies every night.
He dances in his doghouse
till the early morning light.

The other dogs come running
when they hear my doggy swing.
A few will play their instruments.
The others dance and sing.

They pair off with their partners
as their tails begin to wag.
They love to do the bunny hop,
the fox trot, and the shag.

You'll see the doghouse rockin'
as a hundred dogs or more
all trip the light fantastic
on the doghouse disco floor.

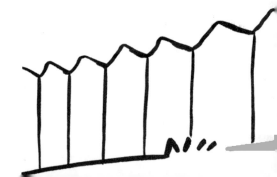

At last, at dawn, they exit
in the early morning breeze,
and stop to sniff the fire hydrants,
bushes, lawns, and trees.

I just don't understand it
for although it looks like fun,
I can't see how they fit inside
that doghouse built for one.

GABBY THE GARBAGE COLLECTOR

I'm Gabby the garbage collector.
I pick up your garbage all year.
It fills me with glee that you'd save it for me.
Collecting's a thrilling career.

I like to get bottles and boxes,
banana peels, bedsprings, and bags.
I'm simply ecstatic with stuff from your attic,
like roasting pans, racquets, and rags.

Your coffee grounds give me the shivers.
I cherish your chicken bones too.
I'm over the moon about half-eaten prunes,
and moldy old vegetable stew.

I'm crazy for custard containers,
and egg cartons brimming with shells.
I love the corrosion, decay and erosion,
and all of the glorious smells.

Your half-empty packets of ketchup,
instill me with chills of delight.
Just one rusted key or a broken CD,
and swiftly my spirit takes flight.

I have the most awesome assemblage.
I treasure each tidbit and lump.
You're welcome to see my collection for free;
it's here on display at the dump.

THE MONSTER MATTRESS SUPERSTORE

The Monster Mattress Superstore
is owned by dear old Fred,
or, as he's better known,
the Monster Underneath Your Bed.

His beds are cold and clammy
just the way a monster likes.
He also offers beds of nails
and mattresses with spikes.

His water beds are filled with sharks,
piranhas, eels, and squids.
But, just in case, Fred also carries
comfy beds for kids.

And Fred makes sure that every mattress
always feels all right
by checking every bed he sells you
EVERY SINGLE NIGHT.

i DON'T KNOW WHAT TO DO TODAY

I don't know what to do today.
Perhaps I'll go outside and play,
or stay indoors and watch TV,
or take a bath, or climb a tree.

Or maybe I'll go ride my bike,
or pick my nose, or take a hike,
or jump a rope, or scratch my head,
or play a game, or stay in bed,
or dance a jig, or pet the cat,
or drink some milk, or buy a hat,
or sing a song, or read a book,
or change my socks, or learn to cook,
or dig a hole, or eat a pear,
or call my friends, or brush my hair,
or hold my breath, or have a race,
or stand around and slap my face.

I'm so confused, and bored, and blue,
to not know what I ought to do.
I guess that I should just ask you.
So, what do you think I should do?

HAP-THE-HAPPY-HYPHENATOR

I'm-Hap-the-Happy-Hyphenator.
Hyphens-are-my-thing.
I-like-the-way-they-give-my-words-
that-extra-bit-of-zing.

I-really-can't-explain-it,-
but-it-makes-me-feel-just-great.
And-so,-no-matter-what-I-write,-
I-always-hyphenate.

I-do-not-like-parentheses.
Quotation-marks-are-dull.
Apostrophes-and-colons-drive-me-
right-out-of-my-skull.

I-do-not-need-the-angle-bracket,-
question-mark-or-slash.
I'd-love-to-stay-and-tell-you-more-
but-now-I-have-to-dash-----

DREAMING OF SUMMER

I'm dreaming of warm sandy beaches.
I'm dreaming of days by the pool.
I'm dreaming of fun in the afternoon sun,
and week after week of no school.

I'm thinking of swim suits and sprinklers,
imagining lemonade stands.
I'm lost in a daydream of squirt guns and ice cream
and plenty of time on my hands.

I'm longing for baseball and hot dogs,
I'm picturing games at the park,
and how it stays light until late every night,
and seems like it never gets dark.

I want to ride skateboards and scooters.
I need to wear T-shirts and shorts.
I'd go for a hike, or I'd ride on my bike,
or play lots of summertime sports.

My revery turns to a yearning
to draw on the driveway with chalk.
It's really a bummer to daydream of summer
while shoveling snow from the walk.

MY ELEPHANT IS MISSING

I cannot find my elephant.
He must have run away.
He isn't on the sofa
where he promised he would stay.

I've looked around the living room,
the kitchen, and the hall.
My elephant is missing
and I'm not sure whom to call.

I'll need to get a bloodhound
who can track him by his scent,
or hire a house detective
to discover where he went.

He isn't in the basement
or the attic or the yard.
You'd think, to find an elephant
would not be quite so hard.

Perhaps I'll make some posters,
and I'll offer a reward.
I'd make it more, but fifty cents
is all I can afford.

If you should see my elephant,
he answers to "Jerome."
Please tell him that I miss him
and I wish he'd come back home.

He knows the way. It's up the street
and down our garden path.
And next time I won't warn him
when it's time to take his bath.

ACKNOWLEDGMENTS

Thank you to all of the kids who took the time to read, rate, and comment on the poems on poetry4kids.com. Your contributions have helped, more than anything else, to select the poems in this book. To my wife, Ann, and my kids, Madison and Max, thank you for your love and support, and for allowing me the time to write and share my poetry with kids everywhere. To my editors, Dominique, Lyron, and Kelly, thank you for helping to make this book as good as it is. You guys rock. To Linda Knaus, who co-authored several of the poems in this book, thank you so much. You are one amazing poet. To Hershey's and Starbucks, thanks for making the writing fuel. A special thanks is due to soundsnap.com for providing the sound effects and music used on the audio CD that accompanies this book. And, perhaps most importantly, thank you to the parents and teachers everywhere who make reading fun for your kids. I hope you enjoy *My Hippo Has the Hiccups*!

INDEX

ABOUT THE AUTHOR

Kenn Nesbitt is possibly the funniest and most sought-after children's poet writing today. When he is not writing, podcasting, updating his website, poetry4kids.com, or visiting schools sharing his wacky brand of humor with kids across America, Kenn and his pet hippo can often be seen exploring the western plains in search of the legendary wild cannoli. Okay. So there's no such thing as a legendary wild cannoli. And Kenn Nesbitt doesn't really have a pet hippo. But he wants one. Especially one that doesn't eat too much. Maybe a pygmy hippo. They're so cute. Don't you agree? Of course you do.

ABOUT THE ILLUSTRATOR

Ethan Long is a children's book author and illustrator whose titles include the extremely popular *Tickle the Duck!* and the hilarious sequel, *Stop Kissing Me!* He was taught how to draw by a wild boar in the deep woods of Pennsylvania. He started out learning with his feet, but eventually his hands grew in and he made the switch. Now look at him. He's a professional artist and loving life. It's a dream come true. "True" being the drawing and the deep woods of Pennsylvania part. Not the part about the wild boar and drawing with his feet. Nor the part about his hands growing in. That's kind of sick.